Unfortunately, She Was Also Wired for Sound

Doonesbury books by G. B. Trudeau

Still a Few Bugs in the System
The President Is a Lot Smarter Than You Think
But This War Had Such Promise
Call Me When You Find America
Guilty, Guilty, Guilty!
"What Do We Have for the Witnesses, Johnnie?"
Dare To Be Great, Ms. Caucus
Wouldn't a Gremlin Have Been More Sensible?
"Speaking of Inalienable Rights, Amy. . ."
You're Never Too Old for Nuts and Berries
An Especially Tricky People
As the Kid Goes for Broke
Stalking the Perfect Tan
"Any Grooming Hints for Your Fans, Rollie?"
But the Pension Fund Was Just Sitting There
We're Not Out of the Woods Yet
A Tad Overweight, but Violet Eyes to Die For
And That's My Final Offer!
He's Never Heard of You, Either
In Search of Reagan's Brain
Ask for May, Settle for June
Unfortunately, She Was Also Wired for Sound

In Large Format
The Doonesbury Chronicles
Doonesbury's Greatest Hits
The People's Doonesbury

a Doonesbury book by

GB Trudeau.

Unfortunately, She Was Also Wired for Sound

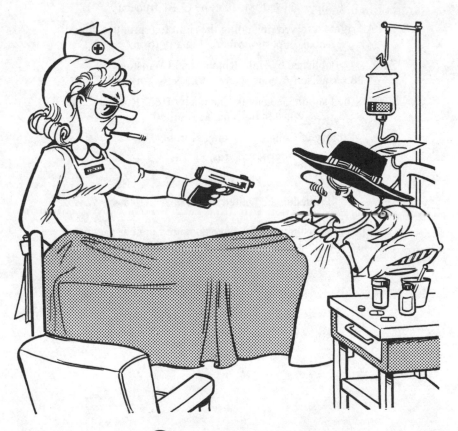

An Owl Book 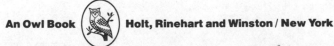 **Holt, Rinehart and Winston / New York**

Published by Holt, Rinehart and Winston, 383 Madison Avenue, New York, New York 10017.

Published simultaneously in Canada by Holt, Rinehart and Winston of Canada, Limited.

Library of Congress Catalog Number: 82-81239

ISBN: 0-03-061731-6

First Edition

Printed in the United States of America

The cartoons in this book have appeared in newspapers in the United States and abroad under the auspices of Universal Press Syndicate.

2 4 6 8 10 9 7 5 3 1

ISBN 0-03-061731-6

YOU REALLY THINK ZONKER'S MAKING A BIG MISTAKE BY RETIRING, DON'T YOU, BERNIE?

DARN RIGHT I DO. IT'S JUST UNCONSCIONABLE. HE'S LETTING A LOT OF PEOPLE DOWN.

WELL, I WOULDN'T BE SO QUICK TO JUDGE, BERNIE. ZONKER'S PAID HIS DUES. HE SWEATED AND BAKED FOR FOUR YEARS OUT ON THAT CIRCUIT, AND HE WON A LOT OF NEW FANS FOR THE SEDENTARY ARTS.

I THINK HE'S ENTITLED TO A CHANGE NOW, BERNIE, AND HE'S ALSO ENTITLED TO OUR SUPPORT. HE'S GOT A BRAND-NEW LIFE AHEAD OF HIM, AND I ADMIRE HIS COURAGE FOR FACING IT SQUARELY!

..AND IT LOOKS LIKE ANOTHER CLEAR, SUNNY WEEKEND, JACK!

MY GOD.. WHAT HAVE I DONE?..

© B Trudeau

AMONG THE RIOTERS WHO FOUGHT POLICE IN THE BLIGHTED TOXTETH DISTRICT OF LIVERPOOL WAS A 17-YEAR-OLD DROP-OUT WHO CALLS HIMSELF "TEDDY SPUTUM."

MR. SPUTUM, WHY DID YOU PERSONALLY PARTICIPATE IN THE RIOTS?

THE BLOODY COPPERS, MAN! WE HATE 'EM! THEY BEEN KNOCKIN' US ABOUT FOR YEARS SO WE GOT EVEN!

ALSO, THERE'S NO BLEEDIN' JOBS, IS THERE? WE GOT NUTHIN TO DO BUT HANG OUT! WITHOUT A JOB, I DON'T HAVE ME SELF-RESPECT!

I SEE. AND WHAT LINE OF WORK WERE YOU INTERESTED IN, MR. SPUTUM?

I DUNNO..MAYBE SOMETHIN' IN THE FASHION INDUSTRY.

GBTrudeau

WE'VE GOT A HEAVY CALL-IN GUEST TONIGHT, TROOPS — SKIP WILLIS, EX-MARINE CAPTAIN AND VIETNAM P.O.W. AS YOU MAY KNOW, SKIP IS HEADING UP THE NEW VIET VET COUNSELLING SERVICE IN TOWN..

A LOT OF VETS STILL NEED HELP BUT DON'T KNOW WHERE TO GET IT. IF YOU'VE GOT QUESTIONS ABOUT THE CENTER — OR IF YOU JUST WANT TO TALK OUT YOUR NAM EXPERIENCES, GIVE US A CALL AT 777-5500!

WELL, SKIP, THANKS FOR DROPPING BY..

HEY, GIVE THEM A CHANCE! IT'S BEEN TEN YEARS!

GBTrudeau

...AND THAD SAYS THAT SECRETARY WATT HAS ALREADY APPROACHED TEXAS ABOUT TAKING BACK THE MATAGORDA WILDLIFE REFUGE!

THAT MEANS DEVELOPMENT, WHICH MEANS THE END OF AN UNDISTURBED HABITAT FOR SEVERAL DIFFERENT ENDANGERED SPECIES!

IT'S OUTRAGEOUS AND UNCONSCIONABLE! AS SECRETARY OF THE MARYLAND AUDUBON SOCIETY, I'M **SERIOUSLY** THINKING OF DEMANDING WATT'S RESIGNATION IN OUR NEXT NEWSLETTER!

WHY, DEAREST! YOU'VE BEEN POLITICIZED!

I HAVE NO CHOICE. PART OF HAVING CLOUT IS NOT BEING AFRAID TO USE IT!

GBTrudeau

SON, BEFORE YOU GET TO JUDGIN' YOUR UNCLE TOO HARSHLY, LET ME TELL YOU SOMETHIN' 'BOUT THIS OLD BOY AND WHAT HE'S DONE FOR US..

THERE AIN'T A FARMER AROUND WHO HENRY AIN'T HELPED ONE TIME OR OTHER. HE'S FIXED OUR BRIDGES, LOANED US COUNTY TRUCKS, EVEN FILLED THE POT HOLES BACK OF THIS BAR!

HENRY KNOWS THE FOLKS AROUND HERE, AND HE'S DONE RIGHT BY US FOR 15 YEARS. YOUR UNCLE MAY BE A CROOK, BOY, BUT HE'S **OUR** CROOK!

SEE, MIKEY? YOU CAN'T **BUY** THAT KIND OF LOYALTY.

NOT ANY MORE, LEAST-WAYS.

UNCLE HENRY, LET'S GO HOME.

.. AND I'M PLEASED TO REPORT TO THE TRUSTEES THAT THANKS TO OUR NEW COST-CUTTING MEASURES, THE UNIVERSITY IS FINALLY BACK ON SOLID FINANCIAL GROUND!

THERE IS AS WELL A NEW ACADEMIC PROSPERITY. RIGOROUS CURRICULUM REQUIREMENTS HAVE BEEN REINSTATED. TEACHERS ARE TEACHING, STUDENTS ARE STUDYING, LIBRARIES ARE FILLED TO CAPACITY!

IN SHORT, LADIES AND GENTLEMEN, A MOST GRATIFYING PICTURE. I'D BE HAPPY TO ENTERTAIN ANY QUESTIONS YOU MIGHT HAVE NOW.

YEAH, KING, HOW COME THE TEAM'S BEEN PLAYING LIKE A BUNCH OF SICK NUNS?

I'LL HAVE TO GET BACK TO YOU ON THAT, PHIL.

GBTrudeau

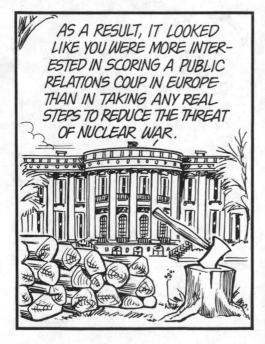